CLYNE CASTLE, SWANSEA.

CLYNE CASTLE SWANSEA

a history of the building and its owners

RALPH A. GRIFFITHS

University College of Swansea 1977

First published March 1977 by the University College of Swansea. Obtainable from The Publications Office, University College of Swansea, Singleton Park, Swansea SA2 8PP.

Copyright © Ralph A. Griffiths 1977

All rights reserved. No part of this publication may be reproduced, stored in a retrieval system, or transmitted in any form or by any means, electronic, mechanical, photocopying, recording, or otherwise, without the prior permission of the Copyright owner.

ISBN 0 86076 001 4

Printed by A. McLay & Co., Ltd., Cardiff

Contents

- The Early Days *13*
- Richard Phillips and the First House at Clyne, 1790–1800 *15*
- George Warde and the Gothic Castle, 1800–30 *17*
- A Critical Interlude, 1830–60 *25*
- The Vivians of Swansea *28*
- The Millionaire of Clyne, 1860–1912 *30*
- The Lady of Clyne, 1912–21 *46*
- The Admiral, 1921–52 *47*
- Town and University *55*
- Conclusion *59*
- Acknowledgements *60*

For

Sally Roberts

Matron of Neuadd Gilbertson, 1961-76

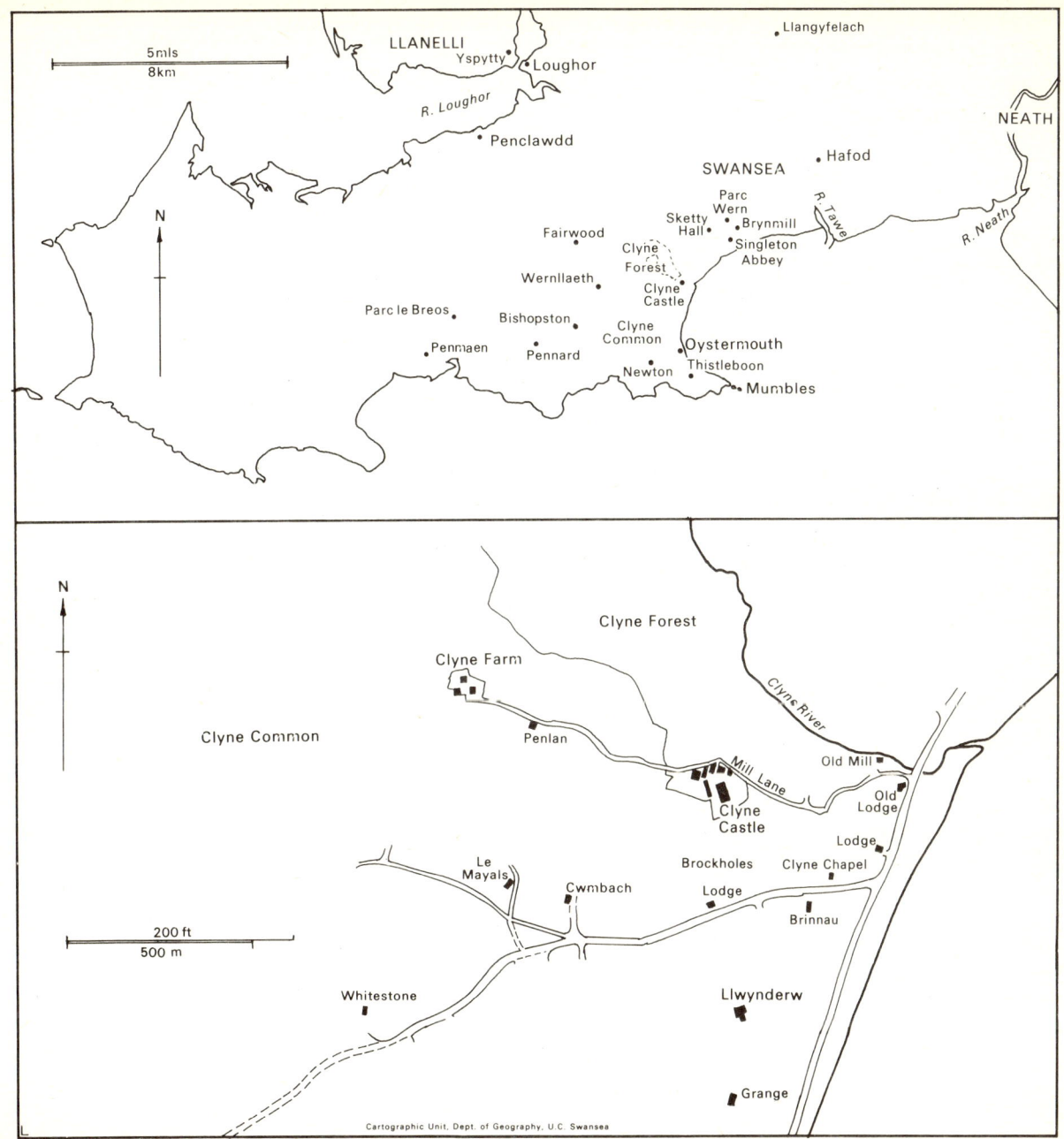

MAP 1 *The Clyne estate and its environs in South Wales*

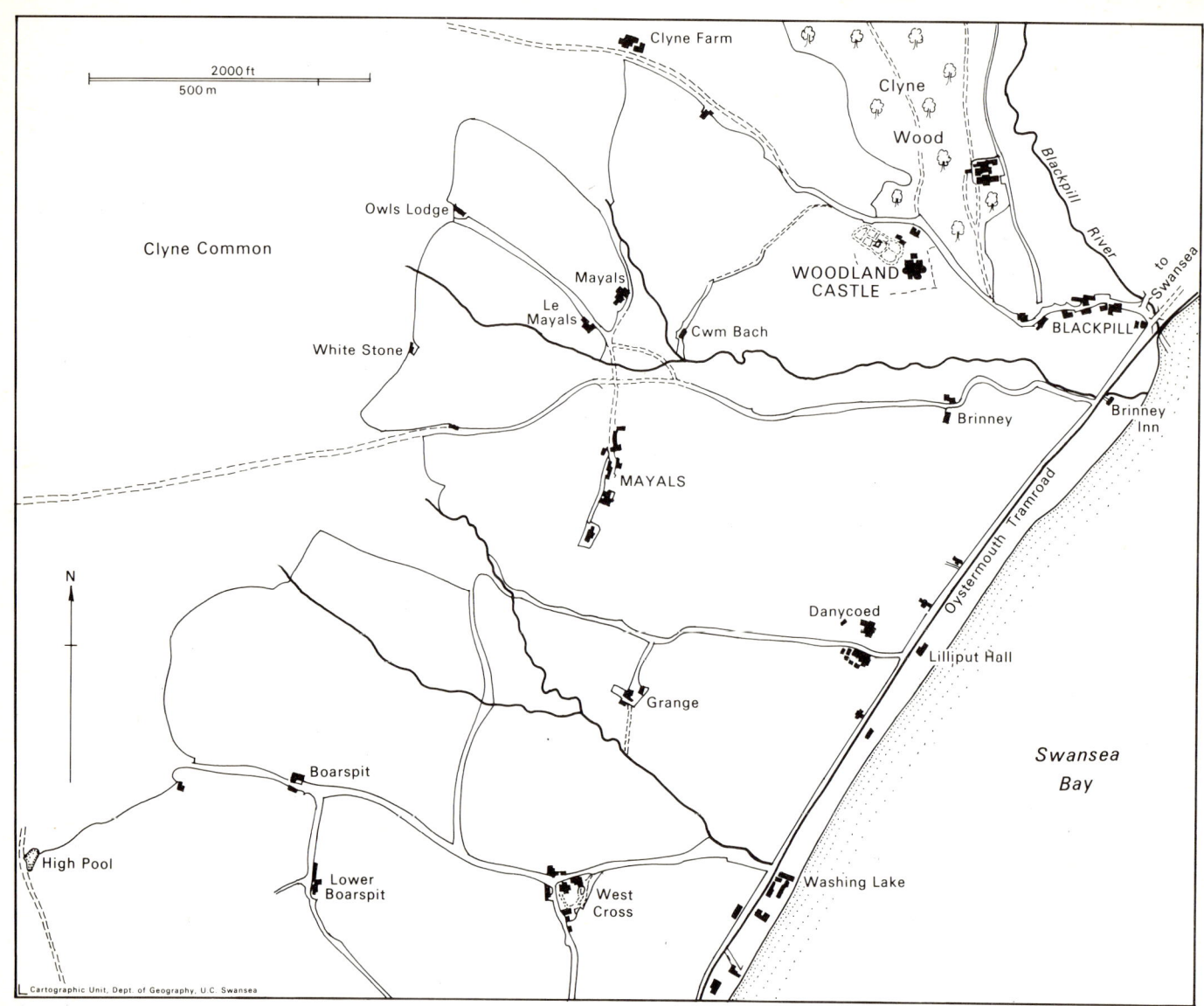

Map 2 *Part of the parish of Oystermouth, as adapted from the Tithe Map of the 1840s. The plan of Woodlands Castle indicates the existence of a west facade similar to that surviving today on the east side of the house; it was demolished in 1860*

The Early Days

With the engaging succinctness of which the Welsh language is capable, 'clun' or (in local parlance) 'clyne' has long been the name given to the slope of woodland and meadow which rises boldly from the western foreshore of Swansea Bay. Clyne Forest was a prominent landmark when the first Normans arrived in Gower at the end of the eleventh century, and together with Clyne Moor or Clyne Common along the crest of the hill it has remained so ever since. Down the centuries, it has supplied timber for building and smelting, and for the shipping industry of the bay; early in the eighteenth century its oaks were being felled by the hundred for British naval dockyards. The forest's veins of coal were probably being dug long before their first record in the seventeenth century and they continued to be worked until 1916. Amidst the trees, an arsenic and naphtha plant was opened and remained a going concern until 1841. In short, the 'clun' has been noteworthy for centuries for its abundant natural resources.

In modern times, Clyne Forest was part of the enormous Gower estate of the earls of Worcester (later to become dukes of Beaufort). That part of it nearest the shore-line was known as Brockholes in 1650 from the little 'brocke' (or brook) which tumbled down beside it. In that year, Walter Thomas of Danygraig leased this 'woody ground', seven acres in extent, for 10s. a year. Walter was a successful coal merchant and substantial landowner at Newton and Thistleboon as well as on the east bank of the River Tawe. A prominent figure in the town of Swansea, he had been its portreeve (the equivalent of mayor) in 1615 and 1625. When the Civil War broke out in 1642, he was resolutely royalist in his sympathies and, despite his advanced age, attempted to hold Swansea castle for King Charles I in 1644–45. He has been described by the Swansea historian, W. H. Jones, as 'a man of much forcefulness of character and local influence, and possessing a breezy enthusiasm in municipal affairs . . .'. For 10s. Walter Thomas can hardly have leased a house at Brockholes, especially when one learns that a water-mill on the Black pill nearby raised as much as £12 in annual rent for the earl of Worcester. There was, then, no house at Clyne in the seventeenth century. The mill, on the other hand, was evidently a substantial building. Renovated from time to time, it occupied the same spot until quite recent times and Mill Lane is still a minor thoroughfare beside the Black pill.

PLATE 1 *The view from the roof of the present Clyne Castle, with Mumbles Head in the distance.*

University College of Swansea

Richard Phillips and the First House at Clyne, 1790-1800

Credit for building the first house at Clyne must go to Richard Phillips. He was, it seems, a younger son of the influential Phillips family of Coedgain, near Carmarthen, which in its time provided M.P.s for Carmarthen Borough and sheriffs for the county. By 1790 Richard had turned his interest to Swansea, where he bought more than 27 acres of land, including Brockholes, 'Le Mayolls' (or the Mayals), and Penlan Wood above. Like Walter Thomas and his son William a century earlier, Phillips was probably attracted by the mineral and timber resources of the property, for when he began to play a part in the town's affairs he did so as a representative of the business and mining community of the Swansea area. As a burgess of the town, he was elected to the newly-formed Board of Trustees of the Harbour, and during the next few years he took a leading role in the harbour's development and the construction of a new light-house at Mumbles.

Prosperous entrepreneurs in the eighteenth century were more likely to build country residences than to live in towns, and in contrast to his predecessors at Clyne, Richard Phillips decided to live on his estate. In 1791 he set about constructing what was described as a 'capital messuage' called 'Woodlands'. The new house was aptly named. Its site was chosen with care, imagination and a keen awareness of the natural beauty of the woodland – so much so that not one of his successors as owners of the estate thought fit to change the position of their residence. It was Richard Phillips who chose this magnificent site. Sheltered by dense, luxuriant woodland, the house in its meadow was open only towards the south, but there the vista extended majestically to the bay – and to Mumbles Head beyond (Plate 1).

Phillips's house was a substantial one, constructed about half a mile from the shore and some 200–300 feet above sea-level. It was built in the simple, regular, almost severe, classical style of the age (Plate 2). The architect was a man called Wyatt, and it is tempting to identify him with one of the prolific family of Wyatts that dominated the architectural scene in Britain in the late-eighteenth and early-nineteenth centuries. In 1791 one of the most prominent of this remarkable family was Benjamin Wyatt, who was well known in north Wales as the agent and architect of Lord Penrhyn. Whether he (or one of his relatives) in fact advised Richard Phillips at Clyne we do not know. But supervision of the practical details of building Woodlands was the responsibility of David Griffith, a mason who probably came from the locality.

Richard Phillips did not enjoy his new residence for long. By 1798 he was dead and his kinsman, James Phillips, had acquired the estate. James lived in London, where he had set up in business as a printer and stationer; his personal interest in Woodlands was, therefore, likely to be far less than that of its builder. Thus, when James too died (in 1799) the decision was taken to sell the property and to sever the Phillips link with it. A ready buyer was to hand, someone who may have learned of the sale in London or (more likely perhaps) was already interested in the developing industrial wealth of the Swansea region and needed a suitable residence there. His name was George Warde.

PLATE 2 *A sketch of Woodlands before George Warde's reconstruction, by 'T.E.'*
Royal Institution of South Wales

PLATE 3 *George Warde, from the portrait by John Opie (1761-1807).*
Mr. John Warde, Squerryes Court, Kent

George Warde and the Gothic Castle, 1800-30

Warde was a forty-year-old colonel in the British Army when he first came to south Wales (Plates 3, 4). Like many experienced and well-to-do Englishmen who moved to Wales during the eighteenth and nineteenth centuries, he was bent on exploiting the mineral and industrial potential of the country. But unlike most of these English entrepreneurs, who had a commercial or industrial background, his career to date had been almost exclusively that of a professional soldier and his family background that of a country gentleman. George was the youngest of the three sons of John Warde of Squerryes Court, Kent, where a branch of the family still lives. He came of well-regarded stock and in January 1781 married Charlotte, the daughter of Spencer Madan, the austere Anglican clergyman who later became bishop of Bristol and eventually bishop of Peterborough (Plate 5). On her mother's side, Charlotte had aristocratic blood in her veins, for she was a granddaughter of the first Earl Cornwallis. Moreover, the marriage was something of a financial *coup* for Warde; the couple received £5,000 from the Cornwallis estate and it was this that partly enabled George Warde to satisfy his ambition to go a-mining in south Wales.

His military career was unexceptionable in its achievements and in the promotion it brought him. He was first commissioned in the 14th Dragoons serving in Ireland in March 1774. Indeed, much of his active service was spent in that troubled island, where his regiment endeavoured 'to redress the indiscipline which has been so much complained of'. He was promoted lieutenant in October 1776 and transferred to the 9th Dragoons; towards the end of 1780, he joined the 2nd troop of Horse Grenadier Guards, of which he became captain in April 1781. Unfortunately for Warde's prospects, this regiment was reduced to a mere cadre in June 1788. As a result, Captain Warde found himself with the luxury of full pay and very few duties to perform – and at a time when Britain was engaged in almost continuous warfare with France. The Grenadier Guards continued to list him as one of their officers until the regiment was actually disbanded in 1808, long after Warde had effectively retired. Nevertheless, he had in the meantime been promoted major in 1790, colonel in 1798 and, finally, while at Swansea engaged in other affairs, major-general on 1 January 1805. It was a common story of gradual promotion in return for modest activity at little risk.

After his marriage Warde lived at Bradfield, near Reading. He was drawn to the Swansea area by its mineral resources. In particular, he was attracted by the mining undertakings of the Townshend family in the coal veins near the Burry estuary in Carmarthenshire, along the eastern bank of the River Loughor. When these came up for sale shortly before 1800, he bought them. For the next thirty years Warde worked the Cwndwnmawr and Golden coal seams; he sank new pits near Llanelli and shipped the coal from Yspytty Bank, near Loughor. His wife's wealth had doubtless enabled him to make this major transition from military to civilian life, and with her money and the expected profits from his industrial ventures he decided to purchase the Woodlands estate from the Phillips family in December 1799.

Once he had moved into Woodlands in 1800, he became absorbed in the commercial and mining development of his new estate and of the Swansea area generally. By the summer of that year, he had built a mill near the increasingly well-known Swansea pottery, situated beside the Strand in the town itself. Not unreasonably, he strenuously opposed the construction of a floating harbour shortly afterwards because he feared that it would harm his commercial enterprises. Indeed, so effective was his opposition that a full generation was to pass before Swansea's floating harbour was completed. The vigorous – some would say intemperate or even deceitful – expression of views displayed in his surviving letters creates an impression of a stubborn and scheming individual. Warde's correspondents among the Stevens family of Bradfield (Berkshire), who were his neighbours, landlord and parish priest before and after the purchase of Woodlands, were involved in interminable arguments with him over tithes, weir rights, his lease of Bradfield House and the propriety of christening his son Henry at home. They are unlikely to have accepted Warde's own assessment of himself: 'tho' I may express myself warmly, I have always previously determined to sleep in charity'.

George Warde quickly established himself as a prominent

PLATE 4 *'Charger', General Warde's horse, mounted probably by the General himself; engraved by John Scott (1774-1828) after Benjamin Marshall (d. 1835).*
National Portrait Gallery

PLATE 5 *Charlotte Warde (née Madan), from the portrait by John Opie (1761-1807).*

British Library

figure in the Swansea area, and he was regarded as well qualified to organise the defence of the locality against invasion by troops from Napoleon's France. Accordingly, on 29 November 1803 he was appointed Inspecting Field Officer of the Swansea yeomanry and volunteer troops, and his headquarters was at Woodlands. Later on, when the king's birthday and the anniversary of the battle of Waterloo (1815) were celebrated, salutes were fired by General Warde from two field cannon which (tradition has it) were captured during the Napoleonic wars and presented to Warde by the Duke of Wellington.

In addition to a possible acquaintance with Wellington, George Warde's contacts were wide and influential. On one occasion, he offered hospitality at Woodlands to William, Duke of Gloucester, popularly known as 'Silly Billy'. The latter stayed with the general for a few days in August 1826 in a set of rooms on the south side of the house which have retained the name of The Gloucester Suite ever since. In south Wales itself he had become a figure with whom local notables were eager to be associated. Some of these links were forged socially through the large family which George and Charlotte Warde brought up in Swansea. Of their five sons and two daughters, some married into prosperous Glamorgan families. William, for example, who was twelve when his father bought Woodlands, married a daughter of Edward Hawkins of Court Herbert, near Neath; and in 1822 a daughter, Mary, married Henry John Grant of the prominent Neath house of The Gnoll.

The house in which Warde entertained his distinguished visitors and reared his family was now a grand and imposing residence, set in an expansive estate. Early in 1800, he had paid £1,800 for Woodlands, During the following thirty years, he extended his estate by substantial purchases of property. In June 1802 he acquired Whitestone on the crest of the Mayals rise. But his greatest acquisition came in May 1825. On that occasion, he bought from the Earl of Jersey part of what had long been known – and still is known – as the Grange (which had once been one of Neath Abbey's granges), Brinnau and Bran's Pit, more than 53 acres in all. The parkland immediately surrounding the house was thereby much enlarged towards the north and west; after 1825 it included acres of woodland replete with rich animal and bird life. Warde's eyes roamed yet further afield. He had already bought Thistleboon House, high above Mumbles Head, a property which, like Whitestone, had belonged to his predecessor at Clyne, Walter Thomas, two hundred years before. Thistleboon was followed by High Pool meadow and some more woodland near Newton.

In all, George Warde had created an estate that was 330 acres in extent.

He turned his attention to Woodlands itself as soon as he had signed the deeds of purchase. By January 1800 it was being referred to as Woodlands Castle, a name appropriate

PLATE 6 *A drawing of Woodlands Castle c. 1818 by Thomas Baxter (1782-1821), who spent the years 1816-19 working at the Swansea Pottery. Notice the new Gothic wing to the rear of the Phillips house.*

Royal Institution of South Wales

PLATE 7 *The east stable and coachhouse as they are today, probably largely unaltered since they were built in 1811.*
University College of Swansea.

to its new, military owner and his plans for its rebuilding in a Gothic fashion reminiscent of medieval fortresses. Within two years the new official guide to Swansea could describe his castle as 'a new house in the Gothic style'. And so it was. According to a memorandum in his own hand which still survives, Warde himself acted as the architect, but to build in the neo-Gothic fashion which had become popular in Britain in recent years must surely have required the advice of a professional architect. Such advice may have been forthcoming from William Jernegan, the Channel Islander who planned many of the larger houses and other buildings in Swansea between 1780 and 1820. Tradition claims that he had a hand in the rebuilding of Woodlands, and it is certainly true that his recent design for the new light-house tower at Mumbles incorporated some neo-Gothic features. Warde's chief mason, on the other hand, was the same David Griffith whom Richard Phillips had employed on a quite different kind of building ten years before.

Woodlands Castle was rebuilt in two main phases: the first in 1800 and the second during 1817–20. To begin with, Warde decided to extend Richard Phillips's house towards the north (Plate 6). That done, the gardens to the rear were laid out in 1805; and the east stable and coachhouse, which still stand today largely unaltered, were finished in 1811 (Plate 7). The most imposing part of the enterprise was undertaken just a dozen years before the general died. He began modestly in 1817 with a west stable (now no longer standing), and in the following year added a range of domestic rooms and offices which were demolished a generation later (Plate 8). Then, in 1819 the final and finest phase of the reconstruction began. The west and east fronts were designed to replace entirely the old Phillips residence, and the first stone of the southern flat-faced tower was laid on 19 April 1819 by the mistress of the house, Charlotte Warde. Current coins of the realm were bricked up in the slim edifice, together with 'some account of the different inhabitants of Swansea Bay at the time' and a genealogy of Charlotte's family tracing her ancestors back to King Edward I and, tapping the imagination, to the Saxons beyond. Much of this frontage, now 150 years old, stands basically unaltered (Plate 9).

Woodlands Castle, a controlled example of the romantic Gothic strain in modern architecture, was constructed in a warm sandstone quarried locally, although dressings were obtained from the Forest of Dean. Its irregular design, with an imposingly curved frontage and slightly protruding west and east fronts, was characteristic of this fashion (Map 2). The castellated walls and towers, and the cannon which Warde placed in the grounds, gave it something of the air of a late-medieval fortress. Inside the present house, the long drawing-room is a resplendent legacy from the general's

PLATE 8 *The seal of General Warde (1809) as it appears on a wine bottle discovered in the cellars of Woodlands Castle.*
Royal Institution of South Wales

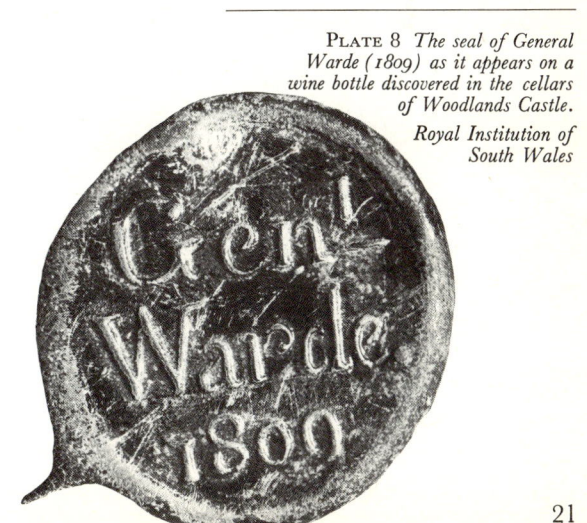

PLATE 9 *The south facade of Clyne Castle as it is today. Apart from the windows and bays inserted in the 1860s, it is much as General Warde built it in 1819-20.*
University College of Swansea

days, and the doorways in the classical style of Robert Adam may date from the same period (Plate 10). Classical interiors often lurked behind the towers, battlements and pointed arches of a neo-Gothic exterior. At that time the grand curvature was punctuated by the main entrance, which led into the centre of the house (Plate 11). The completed castle is portrayed in a well-known engraved lithograph of 1824 (Front cover). It was approached via Mill Lane, at whose junction with the main turnpike road George Warde built a new lodge in a style and stone similar to those of the castle itself. This building, with its pointed window-arches, is easily identifiable today.

This spate of estate- and castle-building was so costly that neither Charlotte's inheritance nor her husband's industrial enterprises could adequately sustain it. As early as 1801, Warde admitted that 'the business in which I am engaged has engrossed every guinea I possessed or could raise; the clauses of my marriage settlements, I believe, empower me to change the security to mortgage, but of course subject to the approval of Trustees'. The Jersey purchase of 1825 forced him within four months into a sizeable mortgage of £6,625. This was still unpaid when Warde died five years later. Moreover, he burnt his fingers badly with the coal mines he had sunk or bought near Llanelli. In 1829, after losing a large sum of money, he sold them to R. J. Nevill, the hard-headed Llanelli industrialist. Some months later, in January 1830, he had to approach Neville for a loan, which was secured by a further mortgage of £2,000 on the Woodlands estate. Repayment was due at the end of one year, but short though this term was, it was too long for Nevill to receive payment before Warde's death. The old general – he was now over seventy – died on 20 June 1830 at Charlton Kings, near Cheltenham. Charlotte survived him by only two years.

George Warde had been an enterprising and farsighted man, one of a breed in south Wales at the turn of the nineteenth century. The rapid industrialisation of the region offered opportunity, wealth and property to such younger sons as he. But Warde had over-extended himself fatally with the variety and size of his industrial and building ventures. The inheritance which passed in 1830 to his eldest son, George, was seriously encumbered with debt and this made it impossible for Wardes to continue to reside at Woodlands Castle in the future.*

PLATE 10 *A doorway after the style of Robert Adam as it appears today in the south-facing wing built by General Warde.*
                                                                University College of Swansea

*By coincidence, a portrait of General Warde's nephew, General Sir Edward Charles Warde, now hangs in the castle. It was presented to the University College of Swansea by Mrs. F. S. Morgan of Bishopston, a grand-daughter of Sir Edward who, however, never lived at Woodlands Castle himself.

PLATE 11 *Woodlands Castle, from a photograph taken about 1841-55 and showing the main entrance in the middle of the south facade of General Warde's house. The pointed window-arches are characteristic of the early-Gothic period (1820).*

National Library of Wales

A Critical Interlude, 1830-60

The financial straits into which George Warde had fallen by the time of his death made it inevitable that Woodlands Castle and its estate would be sold. There stepped forward a man from Monmouthshire who had at his command sufficient finance – and more – with which to buy the outstanding mortgages to the value of over £8,000. Benjamin Hall of Llanover accepted the mortgages in August 1832. His motives are clear. In 1827 his sister, Charlotte Hall, had married Jenkin Davies Berrington, junior, of Swansea, then twenty-six years old and a nephew of General Warde's old agent and attorney, Rhys Davies. Charlotte was the heiress of an estate worth £40,000 and her brother Benjamin acted as her principal trustee and the controller of her wealth. It was her money which was used in 1832 to purchase the mortgages on the Woodlands estate (Plate 12). At first the property was transferred to the elder J. D.

PLATE 12 *Charlotte Berrington (née Hall), the wife of J. D. Berrington junior, from a photograph.* Miss Maxwell Fraser

PLATE 13 *Arthur Berrington (1833-1909) in later life, from a photograph. Miss Maxwell Fraser, with the permission of the late Major J. D. Berrington*

Berrington (who died in May 1834), but the young couple moved into the castle and regarded it as their home. Charlotte, incidentally, was a person of parts, for she shared some of the cultural interests of her sister-in-law, Benjamin's wife. During her time at Woodlands Castle, she put her knowledge of German to work in translating Albert Schulz's 'An essay on the influence of Welsh tradition upon the literature of Germany, France and Scandinavia'; the volume was published in 1841.

The Berrington-Hall connection grew even closer, for Arthur Berrington, Charlotte's son, became the friend, confidant and secretary of Benjamin Hall at a time when the latter was achieving distinction as a minister in Lord Palmerston's government, first as president of the Board of Trade (1854–55) and then as first commissioner of Works (1855–56). It was while he was in the latter post that the clock-tower of the new Houses of Parliament was finished and the bell – 'Big Ben', named most likely after the first commissioner – was heard for the first time. Sir Benjamin was raised to the peerage as Lord Llanover in 1859. Such influential patronage had its drawbacks for Arthur Berrington (Plate 13). Lord Llanover insisted that he stand for

PLATE 14
A sketch of Woodlands Castle as it was at the time of the Berrington purchase (1832).
    Mr. John Warde,
    Squerryes Court, Kent

Parliament and embrace the Liberal cause. Arthur refused. And then there was Lady Llanover. This imperious woman tried to force Arthur (who was already a widower) to marry her protégée, Betha Johnes, the younger daughter and co-heiress of Judge John Johnes of Dolau Cothi, Carmarthenshire. Betha was hopelessly in love with the young secretary, but he refused point-blank to be forced by his uncle's (and employer's) wife into a marriage he did not relish. As a result, uncle and nephew became estranged and Arthur was scathingly denounced by Lady Llanover: 'that most dreaful being', 'scarcely thinking him human', she spat in 1861. Relations were restored only when Lord Llanover lay on his death-bed in 1867.

Arthur had meanwhile been given the Woodlands estate by his father in 1857; within three years it was sold. It is true that between 1834 and 1860 the Berringtons added to the estate in a modest way: a house and property at Blackpill for £116 in October 1837, and the lease of Penlan farm for sixty years in October 1842. But other, more substantial properties along the turnpike road to Oystermouth, which had been acquired by General Warde in 1825, were sold to a Bristol merchant for £1,635 in May 1834. Moreover, in the late-1850s Arthur disposed of some building land at Blackpill on 99-year leases for the ready cash which the Berringtons needed. Indeed, Arthur's father had demolished a major section of the castle, housing sixteen rooms, because the residence was proving too expensive for him to maintain (Plates 14, 15). This probably consisted of the northern wings which Warde had built early in the century. Then, in 1859 Lord Llanover persuaded the Berringtons to move closer to Llanover itself, to Pant-y-Goetre. Benjamin's two sons had died and his daughter had become a Roman Catholic. He therefore contemplated making his likeable nephew and secretary his heir and encouraged him to get to know the Llanover estate. This was more easily done from Pant-y-Goetre than from Swansea. By the end of 1859, therefore, negotiations were under way for the sale of the Woodlands estate to William Graham Vivian of Singleton Abbey. Early in the new year the transaction was completed. Yet Arthur never inherited Llanover because of the bitter family quarrel that soon arose.

PLATE 15
A sketch of Woodlands Castle probably by Lady Llanover before 1857.

Miss Maxwell Fraser

The Vivians of Swansea

One family above all others is associated with the industrial and commercial expansion of Swansea in the nineteenth century. It was the Vivians, more than anyone else, who made the town 'the metallurgical centre of the world'. And their role in the development of the town and port is matched by their towering social position in Swansea and the countryside of Gower. At one time or another during the second half of the century, Vivians occupied the mansions of Singleton Abbey (now part of the University College of Swansea), Park Wern (today the nurses' hostel of Parc Beck), Sketty Hall, Fairwood, Llangyfelach, Parc le Breos and, of course, Clyne.

The Vivians were Cornishmen from the Truro area, and they first acquired their engineering skills and experience in the copper mines of the Cornish peninsula. The sea links between south Wales and the west of England are as old as the channel itself and Cornishmen are no strangers to the Swansea region. Round about 1800, John Vivian arrived as the representative of the 'Associated Miners of Cornwall', who used to ship much of their ore to Swansea for smelting. He set up his own copper works at Penclawdd and a few years later, in 1810, leased land near Swansea where the famous Hafod Works were founded. Meanwhile, in 1806, John's second son, John Henry Vivian, had arrived on the packet boat from Ilfracombe. Although his and his sons' links with Cornwall remained strong, John Henry made his home in Swansea and his fortune in the copper works. He undertook the management of the Hafod Works and was well equipped to do so, for he had been sent by his father to the University of Freiburg and elsewhere in Germany, where the study of mining and mineralogy were making the greatest strides. On his return, be became a friend of the eminent scientists, Michael Faraday and Humphrey Davy. The energy of Vivian, together with his tireless application and inventiveness, ensured success for the factories he owned. The first rolling mill was opened in 1819 and this was followed by the deepening of Swansea's

PLATE 16 *William Graham Vivian (1827-1912) as a young man; from a photograph.*

Royal Institution of South Wales

PLATE 17 *Probably William Graham Vivian (1827-1912), from a portrait by Richard Buckner (fl. 1842-77).*

Mrs. B. Heneage-Williams

harbour to facilitate the import of raw ore and the export of finished copper.

Not far to the west of the town stood a small country house known as Marino; this was bought by John Henry as his home. The family's new-found wealth enabled him to reconstruct it completely, and one of the most fashionable architects of the day, P. F. Robinson, was engaged from 1823 in designing a large mansion in the popular neo-Gothic style – a residence to which Vivian gave the romantic name of Singleton Abbey. John Henry sired a veritable dynasty of Swansea industrialists who were regarded as patricians in the community. His eldest son, bearing the good Cornish name of Hussey, was born in Swansea in 1821; as a young man of twenty-four, he took over management of the Vivian works from his busy father. The other sons, William Graham, Arthur Pendarvis and Richard Glynn, likewise played a prominent (and profitable) part in the family business – especially Graham.

After the death of his father in 1855, Graham may have found himself in an increasingly irksome position at Singleton. His elder brother Hussey still lived at Parc Wern, even though he was now head of the family. Graham and Glynn continued to live at Singleton with their mother, who had been left the house for life by her husband. It is true that Graham would eventually inherit Parc Wern whenever his elder brother moved into Singleton, but their mother showed no sign of expiring (she in fact died in 1886). By 1859 Graham, who was then thirty-two, may have felt the need for a home of his own sooner rather than later (Plates 16, 17). Woodlands Castle fitted the bill. Its simple and more dignified display of neo-Gothicism perhaps appealed to his refined taste more positively than the heavier, extravagant achievements of P. F. Robinson at Singleton. Its spacious rooms and extensive park would enable him to indulge his cultural, aesthetic and rustic interests unhindered, and to pursue the life of an independent gentleman.

The Millionaire of Clyne, 1860-1912

William Graham Vivian had as great an impact on Clyne as General Warde. From the moment he purchased the Woodlands estate in 1860, he lavished attention, money and a sophisticated taste on the castle, converting it into a noble residence stuffed with antiques and *objets d'art* of astonishing variety and value. The castle and its grounds became a by-word for opulence and Graham Vivian renowned for his wealth.

Born in 1827, Graham was a strange, withdrawn and, for his age, eccentric figure. As a child, it was said of him that he was 'a fine stout fellow and chatters famously', but when he was six his eyes were badly affected by a flash of lightning and for some years he could not bear strong light or read very much. Whether this had any deep or lasting effect on the boy is unknown, but he certainly grew up to be a recluse as far as the people of Swansea were concerned. He played little part in public and town affairs, and rarely attended social or other functions in south Wales.

His conservative cast of mind and industrialist's instincts made him a severe employer in the Vivian enterprises. On one occasion, he wrote with some relief to his brother Hussey that 'I am so glad there is a chance now for us to reduce the colliers' wages'. The threat of a coal strike in 1892 and proposals for a better sliding-scale for colliers' wages in Wales simply hardened his attitude: 'Why coal owners or any employers are not to decide for themselves what wages they can afford to give, I cannot see'. Not surprisingly, perhaps, the social reform proposals of Asquith's Liberal government filled him with distaste, and the creeping powers acquired by local authorities offended his landowner's mentality. On the other hand, it was not conservatism but rather a profound concern for the quality of the environment which led him to oppose Swansea's sewage schemes at Brynmill and Mumbles; in 1893 he and his brother Hussey were prepared to use their considerable influence at Westminster to defeat proposals which, in Graham's view, would pollute Swansea Bay. Only in his later years did he emerge from his apparent shell and show more sympathetic interest in the Vivians' adopted town. Sometime before his death in 1912, he was elected to the Swansea Dock Authority as one of its Proprietary Trustees, perhaps to replace his elder brother Hussey, who had died in 1894. He also joined the Gower Board of Guardians at about the same time. One of his last public appearances was in July 1911 at the opening of the Swansea Art Gallery, which he named after its principal benefactor, his younger brother Glynn. In his will, Graham offered a handsome £10,000 to Swansea Hospital which was devoted to the construction of the 'Graham Vivian Ward', just as the donor had directed in a last act of self-esteem. But this was the only substantial public gift known to have been made by him in Swansea. Extraordinary, too, in a man of surpassing skill in industry and commerce was his refusal to avail himself of some of the great discoveries of modern engineering. He refused to buy a motor-car and throughout his life preferred to be driven by his favourite pair of chesnut horses. He declined to have a telephone installed at Clyne, a decision which raised problems for his doctors when his final illness struck in 1912.

Equally uncommon for his age was his concern for the environment and his dedication to its protection against unrestrained exploitation by urban and industrial expansion. The preservation of the last remaining kites in Britain was a particular concern of Graham Vivian, and he became a vigorous opponent of those who would vandalise the countryside in the name of progress or profit. It was a trait present in his father, for all John Henry's determination to expand the Hafod Works; but in Graham Vivian it was extraordinarily finely developed. The tenant who leased the nearby Llwynderw property from Graham was sharply dealt with in 1901 when he began cutting down some of the old trees. 'I have had quite experience enough of the mania which grows upon some people for cutting, in my late brother [Lord Swansea] and my cousin Mr. Webber, who got leave from Mr. Morris to cut what trees he liked at Glynderw and ruined the little place.' He was truly incensed in 1908 when a new lessee began unauthorised cutting at Llwynderw 'beyond what I could have conceived possible'; he promptly took the man to court.

In its obituary of him, *The Western Mail* described Graham as a man of a somewhat retiring disposition and 'without ambition to be a leader of men'. In a public and local sense the newspaper was correct, for Graham showed no desire to cut a popular figure in the Swansea area; but in other respects, it was a misleading judgement. There can be no doubt that Graham was a financier and businessman of genius. His local reputation for meanness was simply a superficial reflection of the thrift and careful supervision he practised as a principal shareholder of Vivian and Sons Ltd., and in other ventures; even in his late seventies he retained a crystal-clear grasp of business detail. When he died in 1912 he was a millionaire. His estate was estimated to be worth more than £1⅓ million, almost 90 per cent of it derived from his business interests and investments. His share of the family firm was valued at more than £½ million, for not long before Graham had purchased the share of his nephew, Lord Swansea, 'to save it falling into other hands' – an expensive determination to preserve the family's control over the Vivian firm.

It is sometimes said of Graham that he was jealous of his elder brother and therefore refused to participate in the new ventures which Hussey had in mind in the 1880s and early-1890s. It is true that they quarrelled over their father's will in 1856, that Graham in 1883 withdrew an earlier promise to invest in H. H. Vivian and Company 'in a very unhandsome letter', and that in 1893–4 he refused to allow Vivian and Sons to be amalgamated with other firms. But the surviving letters between the brothers show them to have been almost always friendly and affectionate towards one another (as far as anyone could be who always signed himself 'W. Graham Vivian'). It was Graham's philosophy that ties of blood should not confound business judgements. By the 1880s it is likely that Graham foresaw that the heavy extractive industries of the Swansea area had seen their most prosperous days and were entering a period of decline. Yet there can be no doubting his deep sense of responsibility for the family firm, as the purchase of his nephew's share proves. When Arthur's neglect of his responsibilities in the business reached a head in 1880, Graham was as forthright as Hussey in reprimanding their brother. This experience doubtless reinforced his innate hard-headed business ethics, for when it was proposed a few

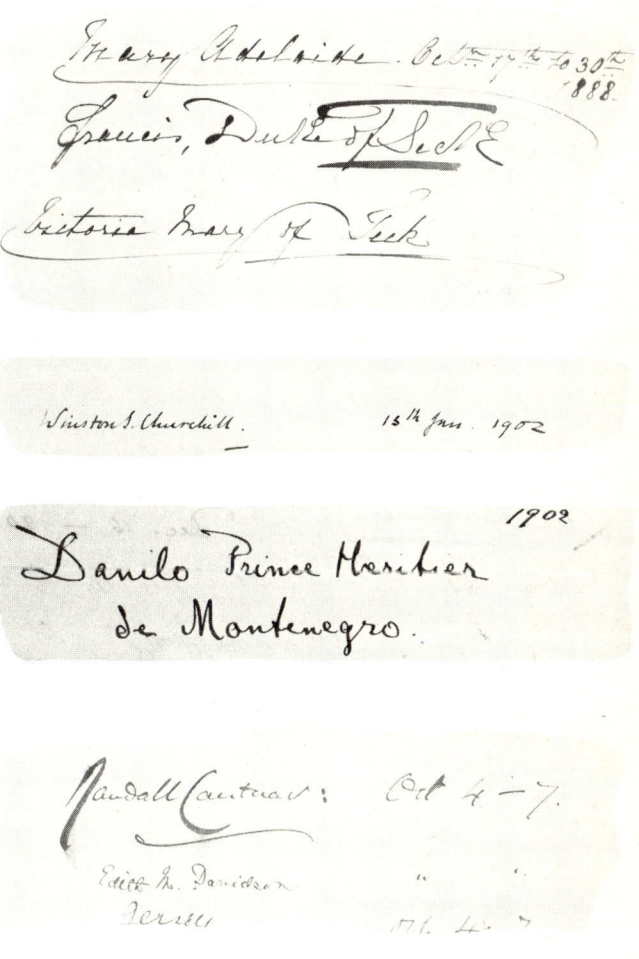

PLATE 18 *From the Visitors' Books of Clyne Castle.*

Mrs. B. Heneage-Williams

years later to introduce another relative to the Hafod Works, Graham smartly dismissed the idea without a trace of sentiment: 'I think it never desirable to have relatives as agents . . . one can never get rid of them . . .' He liked the young man concerned, but business was business!

To add to his cherished wealth, Graham purchased mortgages worth £110,000 on property scattered in London, the home counties and the midlands, as well as in Swansea. Yet the core of his fortune was a series of shrewd investments made the world over, particularly in railway companies in north, central and south America, Britain and Turkey. For all his reluctance to see steam engines and the Mumbles Railway rattling through his property at Blackpill, Graham far-sightedly appreciated the enormous impact which the railway would have on newly industrialised countries and continents. Such wealth gave him influence and he was fully prepared to use it – not to secure public recognition or to enter public service, but rather to pursue those interests which he regarded as important in his life.

He was high sheriff of Glamorgan on only one occasion, in 1868, and to be elected a J.P. and deputy-lieutenant of the county was the minimum expected of a man in his position. However, he enjoyed good company and conversation, and was not without a sense of humour (to judge by his willingness to be photographed in fancy dress). He remained throughout his life a friend or acquaintance of the greatest in the land. He often attended the courts of

PLATE 19 *The visit of the Tecks to Clyne Castle in 1888. The group includes Graham Vivian (third from the left), Dulcie Vivian (extreme right) and their brother Glynn (rear left), the Duke of Teck (fifth from the left), Princess Mary (rear right) and the portly duchess, H.R.H.*

Mrs. B. Heneage-Williams

PLATE 20
The northern end of the north-east wing built by Graham Vivian in the 1860s in a style similar to that of General Warde's house. The photograph was taken in 1952 and shows some of the fine gardens immediately behind the house.

Western Mail

Queen Victoria and King Edward VII, and remained for many years the king's friend. He was regularly in London at his house in Belgrave Square, and was a welcome member of shooting-parties on estates throughout the length and breadth of the country. His roll-call of visitors to Clyne and Parc le Breos for the famous shoots tells the same story. In 1881 the prince and princess of Wales, who were in Swansea to open the new dock, were taken from Singleton Abbey by Sir Hussey to visit his brother at Clyne, and this may have been the beginning of the friendship between Graham and Prince Edward. Lord Palmerston and Lord Cardigan, the Duke of Athol, the Earl of Rosebery, the Duke and Duchess of Teck (with their daughter, later Queen Mary), and scores of English and foreign notables slept at the castle as Graham's guests (Plate 18). The famous opera singer, Adelina Patti, travelled regularly to Clyne with her husband from their home at Craig-y-Nos to take part in the Clyne shoots. These visitors provided Graham with a circle of acquaintances and a position in society which Swansea people rarely appreciated fully. After Prince Edward became king in 1901, he presented Graham with busts of himself and his queen, Alexandra, as a token of their earlier friendship. This stream of high-ranking personages at times taxed the resources of the castle. Before the arrival of the Tecks for a two-week stay in October 1888, Graham was given 'a little *private* information' by an equerry. Her Royal Highness and the duke never put in an appearance before lunch and, since 'they are generally half an hour late for all meals and take an immense time over them', care needed to be taken lest the autumnal days slip by without being noticed! As to rooms, '... the Duke does not care to be too near H.R.H. neither does Princess Mary'. As to wines, a special anti-gout vintage was invariably chosen for H.R.H. (Plate 19).

PLATE 21 *A pointed window from General Warde's building which survived the alterations of the 1860s.*
University College of Swansea

PLATE 22
A painting (of about 1881) of the castle after Graham Vivian's alterations. Notice the conservatory (left front), the new square casement-windows and bays. The new wing and doorway are to the right. Compare plate 9.
*University College of Swansea,
from* A series of Picturesque Views of Seats of Noblemen and Gentlemen of Great Britain and Ireland, *Vol. V (n.d.)*

The castle in which these distinguished visitors stayed reached its present proportions under Graham Vivian. When completed, it had upwards of 50 rooms. In 1860, he was told by Arthur Berrington that a sixteen-room part of General Warde's house (probably the oldest part to the north and west which had housed the castle's domestic quarters) had been demolished as an economy measure. Shortly after becoming its owner, he proceeded to rebuild on this site in a massive way, adding the Great Hall and the north-east wing. The style of architecture, though more solid and dour than that of Warde, nevertheless preserved the neo-Gothic features of the earlier house and in a similar sandstone (Plate 20). There is a suggestion that Graham enlisted the services of Sir Mathew Digby Wyatt, the distinguished architect who was related to the famous Wyatts, had been secretary of the Great Exhibition of 1851 and came to live at Cowbridge in the vale of Glamorgan. At the same time, most of the original pointed window-arches, so characteristic of the first decades of the Gothic Revival, were replaced by the squarer lines of the present

PLATE 23 *(Left) The ceiling of the Great Hall built by Graham Vivian, after Knole House (Kent).*
University College of Swansea

PLATE 24 *(Top) The ceiling of the long drawing-room after Graham Vivian's alterations, after Knole House (Kent).*
University College of Swansea

casements (Plate 21, for a survivor). The line of the magnificent south face was broken by two series of bay windows (Plate 22). Inside, Graham Vivian so designed the formal rooms that his titled visitors would be in familiar surroundings. The ceiling of the lofty hall was copied from Knole (in Kent), whilst Holland House in Kensington was the model for the dining-room ceiling (Plate 23). It was he who converted the original entrance and its adjoining rooms into the long drawing-room, and inserted the graceful ceiling, again after Knole (Plate 24). A serious fire in 1896 does not seem to have damaged these features in any way, although the renovations cost some £2,000.

The rooms themselves were well-nigh unique in character. Their contents show Graham to have been a cultured gentleman whose aesthetic tastes were matched by enormous wealth. Educated at Eton, as a young man he had spent a year in France, perfecting his knowledge of the language, broadening his horizons, and then undertaking 'the grand tour' in eighteenth-century style. Years later, when his brother Hussey was planning a visit to France, Graham eagerly gave him detailed and informed advice on where to go and what to see in Paris and the Loire Valley. His interest in Europe and in travel remained compulsive for many years, and his gift for languages enabled him to

PLATE 25 *The fireplace of the Great Hall built by Graham Vivian. Notice the rare Sevillian tiles.*
University College of Swansea

Florence (Plate 28). The long curved drawing-room, in many ways the pride of the house, was 75 feet long and housed valuable paintings by Sir Peter Lely, Watteau, George Morland and Sir Edwin Landseer, as well as a writing table acquired after the sack of the palace of the Tuileries during the Revolution of 1848 (Plate 29).

speak German and Italian, as well as French, fluently. From his travels and through his contacts he returned with crates bulging with artistic treasures. In the Great Hall were placed wall friezes from an Italian palace, a series of old masters (a Veronese among them), and a fireplace inlaid with rare Sevillian tiles (Plate 25). The dining-room in his new wing was resplendent with huge Gobelin tapestries depicting scenes from Greek mythology; its doors and surrounding oak panels were brought from the archbishop of Paris's palace on the Ile St. Louis (Plate 26). The room's marble mantlepiece (since removed) came from a Dutch castle and was purchased by Graham from one of his acquaintances, Ferdinand de Rothschild. Around the walls were scattered marble busts and pillars from the Roman villa at Cuma and the ruins of Pompeii and Carthage, while one of the tables had come from the Neapolitan palace of the prince of Salerno (Plate 27).

The tapestry drawing-room, the only major room to have been demolished in 1955, was famed for its wall tapestries, again priceless Gobelins. The ceiling was partly covered by a large painting brought from the Medici palace in

PLATE 26 *The oak door of the dining-room, acquired by Graham Vivian from the archbishop of Paris's palace.*
University College of Swansea

PLATE 27 *The dining-room as it was in 1952, with Graham Vivian's tapestries in full view, the oak doors from Paris and the Dutch mantlepiece.*

Mrs. C. D. Fraser Jenkins

PLATE 28 *The tapestry drawing-room as it was in 1952, with Graham Vivian's tapestries and the ornamental ceiling.* Mrs. C. D. Fraser Jenkins

PLATE 29 *The long drawing-room as it appeared in 1952, essentially as it had been in Graham Vivian's day.* Mrs. C. D. Fraser Jenkins

PLATE 30 *One of the marble doors into the long drawing-room, brought from an Italian palace by Graham Vivian.*
University College of Swansea

The grand staircase descended below stained glass from the hand of the renowned sixteenth-century French glass painter and potter, Bernard Palissy. The hallway from the entrance to the Great Hall was inlaid with a mosaic pavement from Carthage. Its marble doorways into the long drawing-room were from yet another Italian palace (Plate 30). Elsewhere items came from a Turkish palace at Constantinople, and in one of the bedrooms was a bed from Beaurepaire in which Queen Elizabeth I really had slept. It was a breath-taking museum of antiques, but a museum that was much frequented by guests and constantly in use by Graham and his friends. Among the true glories of the house were its china and silverware. Graham had a passion for porcelain. He purchased or was given countless pieces of Chinese, Dresden, Sèvres, Worcester, Derby and Chelsea, as well as unique items from Swansea and Nantgarw; some of the latter had been acquired by his father when the potteries were at the height of their fame. Ten pieces of Clyne's finest Swansea and Nantgarw were bought by the Town Council in 1952 and may now be seen in the Glynn Vivian Art Gallery (Plate 31). Graham's taste – as reflected in the tapestries, many of the paintings, some of the china, and the books in his library – was strongly classical, though neither the paintings as a collection nor the library would now be thought distinguished. The former express the strong classical and religious convictions of Graham Vivian, as well as the pride in family and the concern for the natural beauty of Swansea which can be detected in his scores of watercolours of the bay and Gower peninsula. The books were modest in number and conventional in tone, including history, travel, memoirs and classical authors who were popular in the late-nineteenth century; the great novelists like Dickens were on the shelves in illustrated editions, while P. F. Robinson's neo-Gothic designs had more than academic interest for Graham Vivian. But the china, silverware and furniture (some of it from the France of Louis XV and Louis XVI) were justly famous. They were all personal collections of Graham Vivian. This was recognised by the Duke of Teck who, on learning of the fire of 1896, commiserated with his erstwhile host and acknowledged 'how much you valued what you had brought together and created'.

Vivian's London home, 7 Belgrave Square, was situated in the most fashionable area of the capital, and it reflects on a smaller scale the quality of life enjoyed by Graham and his friends. Watercolours by the south Wales artist patronised by the Vivians, James Harris, were reminders of Clyne Park, Singleton and the Gower coast; the porcelain was part of Graham's unique collection; and a priceless Beauvais tapestry on the stairs complemented the Gobelins at Clyne.

The gardens and parkland surrounding Clyne Castle were no less remarkable. In 1871 the Swansea Town Guide lyricised on the climate of Clyne, sheltered as it was by the lee of the Mayals hill: 'as genial . . . as could be found at Malaga or Marseilles'; protected on all sides bar the south, the castle 'nestled in sunshine uninterrupted, save by the

PLATE 31 *A Cabinet Cup and Saucer showing Jubal with his harp; painted by Thomas Baxter, it is 'perhaps the most noted of all pieces of Swansea china' and was part of Graham Vivian's collection.*

Glynn Vivian Art Gallery

o'er clouded canopy'. The exaggeration to which Swansea's natives are sometimes prone was only slight. To this favoured spot, Graham Vivian introduced a range of exotic bushes and trees from as far afield as the Himalayas which have made of Clyne a park of extraordinary richness, variety and wonder, and unique in the Wales of its day. Arbutus, camellia, a eucalyptus growing fifty feet in height close to the house, and a crucifixion thorn supposedly from the Garden of Gethsemane – these are some of the plants which Vivian carefully acquired and nurtured in the large conservatory that stood beside the long drawing-room (Plate 32). And it was he who supervised their planting about the house and grounds with a studied informality that utilised the natural contours of the landscape (Plate 33). Most of them still bloom today. To the west of the house roamed a herd of deer. Once a year Graham opened his grounds to the public; today they are permanently available to the citizens of Swansea.

Towards the end of his life, as he entered his eightieth year, Graham conceived the idea of building a chapel on his estate in which he and his successors could be buried.

In 1860 he had acquired a pew in Oystermouth Church as part of the Berrington sale, but a chapel at Blackpill itself would provide the final proof – if such were needed – that the Vivians were indeed lords of Clyne. Graham was a staunch Anglican by conviction – even to the point of disinheriting in his will any of his designated successors who were received into the Roman Catholic Church. Moreover, when ritualistic tendencies of a high-church variety showed themselves at St. Mary's, Swansea, in 1880, Graham supported his brother Hussey in refusing to contribute to the church's restoration fund. The Vivian Chapel at Clyne bears the stamp of the notable eccentric who was its builder (Plate 34). Graham ensured that no religious novelties were introduced by specifying in his will that the legacy intended to meet the curate's stipend should only be paid 'so long as the services in my said Chapel are held in the manner as at present conducted'. Again, at Graham's precise instruction, the chapel does not follow the usual plan of facing east, and in its tiny chancel and nave he placed some of the European treasures that filled his house. These were all Christian in inspiration. An early mosaic from the church of San Bartholomew in Rome was placed in the wall; the altar was constructed of Sicilian marble; its six candlesticks came from Siena, and the pulpit was once used in Renaissance Rome. A Spanish bell and Portuguese chalice complete its exotic furnishings. The chapel opened for worship in 1908, and was attended in particular by the tenantry of the estate; beneath, in a private vault, Graham Vivian and his two successors at Clyne, his sister Dulcie and nephew Algernon, were duly buried.

By the time of his death, Graham was known as 'The Squire of Clyne'. It was a role he had consciously cultivated for decades. The building of the chapel was one expression of it. Another was the name he gave to his mansion, Clyne Castle, in about 1870, soon after his extensions had been completed. It harked back to the medieval past and emphasised the squire-tenant relationship that figured so prominently in Graham's mind. The creation of an extensive and well-rounded estate was part of the same vision. During his years at Clyne, he gradually made himself the freeholder of almost every property that stood close to his castle and park until, by the beginning of the twentieth

PLATE 32 *The south-west angle of Clyne Castle about 1910, with Graham Vivian's conservatory and woodcocks in the foreground.*   Mr. E. G. Wright

PLATE 33 *A view of some of Graham Vivian's plants still in Clyne Park today.*   Mr. R. Davies, The Guildhall, Swansea

century, he was indeed the squire of a community of tenants centred on the village of Blackpill, looking to the castle as the manor house and to Graham as their squire; eventually, they were able to worship with him in his chapel.

The first major acquisition of land after the initial purchase of 1860 was made in May 1866, when Clyne Farm, which stood some distance further up the hill, was bought. In May 1873 a stretch of land at the bottom of the hill near the foreshore, known as The Gorses at Blackpill Burrows, was also purchased, along with Tremore Cottage; later in the year, other land in the same area was acquired together with Bayswater Cottage. Graham had already spent £220 in June 1870 for other property in Blackpill, and £600 for yet more (including two cottages near the new railway line) in October 1871.

Some of his purchases were of properties which had originally belonged to General Warde but had been disposed of by Arthur Berrington. Thus, houses which had been built on land leased in 1858 were now, in May 1877,

PLATE 34 *The Clyne Chapel built by Graham Vivian in 1907.* *University College of Swansea*

bought for £275, exactly the rent payable during the remainder of their ninety-nine-year lease. The occupiers became Graham's tenants. Three houses in Woodlands Terrace, on the sea-ward side of the main coast-road, had been built on land leased from Berrington; in July 1900 Graham bought their lease for £400, this time paying far more than the total rent payable during the remainder of the lease – so anxious was he to preserve the integrity of the Clyne estate.

In 1819 the Duke of Beaufort had let some land for building on the sea-ward side of the main turnpike. Two houses were constructed on marshy ground near Brinnau Lane, one to be used as an inn (known as Brinney Inn in 1831 and The Woodman by 1880), and the other as a schoolhouse. These were both sold to Vivian in July 1880 for £200. Nearby on the same land there were nine other houses which Vivian took steps to acquire. He succeeded with all but two of them between 1895 and 1901. The licence of The Woodman had meanwhile been transferred across the turnpike road to its present home; the houses,

44

in what was known as Brooklands Terrace, have all been demolished. By 1900, therefore, virtually the whole of Blackpill was a Vivian village, with Graham as its squire. He replaced Mill Lane with a new imposing driveway to the castle. Beginning a little to the west of Warde's lodge, it displayed the glories of the gardens and park more strikingly to the visitor and directed his attention to the fine facade ahead. A new lodge was constructed at the entrance to this drive (perhaps in the 1860s when the castle was extended), and a subsidiary one was placed on the western edge of the estate, near the road leading to Clyne Common.

Further afield, Graham's purchases were more substantial. In February 1897 he secured the farm known as Cwmbach, just off the Mayals, for £2,050; in 1901 it was the turn of the Llwynderw estate, a short distance along the road to Oystermouth, for £10,500. In Bishopston, Wernllaeth farm was bought in July 1904 for £560, and another property at Pennard in July 1908 for £520. The Woodlands estate sold by Arthur Berrington in 1860 had included ninety-seven acres of land; when Graham made his last purchase in 1908 the Clyne estate was more than fifteen times as large. Graham vigorously defended his position as a landlord, preferring to appear himself in the county court in 1885 rather than allow his weir and fishing rights in the stream at Blackpill to be ignored.

His motive in still amassing property when he was well over eighty may be presumed to be a sense of dynasty. Although never marrying, he had a highly developed concern for the name of Vivian and the survival of the estate which he, single-handedly, had created. His carefully constructed will puts it plainly. Graham was determined that his estate should prove viable in the immediate future and preserve its independence even of other Vivian estates like that of his nephew, Lord Swansea, at Singleton. For these reasons, in his will of 1909 he refrained from dividing up the property and from leaving any of it to Lord Swansea. Of his sisters, only the youngest, Dulcie, had not married; she and Graham were devoted to one another, and she was at his side when he died on 21 August 1912. Graham's first and immediate task was to transfer the whole estate to her for life. But if the Vivian line were to continue at Clyne, other arrangements had to be made. He decided to leave the entire estate, after Dulcie's days, as a life trust to Algernon, a younger son of his sister Henrietta and her husband, Major Clement Walker-Heneage, and then to Algernon's male heirs. Should they eventually fail, Graham provided that his estate should go to other of his male relatives in turn. His choice of heirs was largely dictated by their suitability to act as the squire of Clyne. For one thing, whoever succeeded was required to adopt the name and arms of Vivian within one year of acquiring the inheritance. And as far as possible, Clyne should be their prime concern. Algernon, as a younger son, was certainly unlikely to succeed to the Walker-Heneage estate at Compton Bassett in Wiltshire, and so it proved. Graham Vivian could die secure in the knowledge that there was every likelihood of his inheritance surviving intact during the twentieth century.

One week after returning from London, Graham Vivian began to experience severe internal pains on 18 August 1912. He had only been out once, on a drive to Parc Wern. On the 19th he was operated on by Dr. Brooke from Swansea, who had to sleep overnight at Clyne because Graham had never allowed a telephone to be installed. The patient grew increasingly restless and feverish, and on the afternoon of the 21st his grave condition brought Lord Swansea to his bedside from Singleton Abbey. After sitting with his uncle for a few hours, he left by car to return home but was summoned again shortly afterwards with the news that Graham Vivian had died.

The oldest and wealthiest surviving Vivian was apparently popular with his tenants and servants. Although habit and the obligations of Edwardian society were strong sentiments among them, their attendance at his funeral in Clyne Chapel is a striking testimony to their sense of loss. The coffin was made by an old man from Sketty who had done the same service for Vivians since John Henry's day. The funeral procession from the castle, where Graham had lain in the long drawing-room since his death, was headed by the tenantry, one and all carrying wreaths. An array of Vivians and Heneages followed, led by Lord Swansea and Algernon; then came civic leaders including the mayor of Swansea, the town clerk, Glamorgan's official representatives and Lord Glantawe. But Graham had himself ensured that this was not to be the end of an era for Clyne or its castle.

The Lady of Clyne, 1912-21

Dulcie Charlotte Vivian became mistress of Clyne in old age and lived at the castle for barely nine years more. During this brief period, she fulfilled the expectations of the locality as a revered lady and public benefactress (Plate 35). Dulcie occupied the Clyne estate as a life tenant. She had been left £5,000 in her father's will in 1855, and £12,000 by Graham Vivian in 1912. At her death her fortune, much of it inherited from her brother, was put at rather more than £$\frac{1}{2}$ million.

Dulcie never married. She interested herself in the welfare of her tenants, and in charitable and philanthropic work in the town. During the First World War, her house at Penmaen was given to Swansea Hospital so that the war-wounded could be cared for there; later on, she facilitated its permanent transfer to the hospital on advantageous terms. Her other interests included the rest-home for the blind which her brother Glynn had founded at Caswell to help those afflicted with the blindness which had overtaken him in later life.

In 1921 she was making preparations for her regular Whitsun visit to Clyne when, following a short illness, she died at her London home at an advanced age characteristic of the Vivians – eighty-two. Her coffin was drawn by some of the oldest tenants on the estate to the vault in the Vivian Chapel which Graham had built. Like her brother, she had no heirs of her own, and that is why Graham had arranged for the entire estate to pass to their nephew, Algernon, on whom the obligation to continue the Vivian line at Clyne and preserve the integrity of the estate was now laid.

PLATE 35 *Dulcie Charlotte Vivian (left) with her sister Henrietta, the mother of Admiral Walker-Heneage-Vivian.*

Mr. C. Fraser Jenkins

The Admiral, 1921-52

The inheritance into which Algernon Walker-Heneage entered in 1921 was far beyond the normal expectations of a younger son. Born on 4 February 1871, the third son of Major Clement Walker-Heneage and Henrietta Vivian, he could expect to inherit little of the Wiltshire estates of his father. But this very fact made him eminently suitable in Graham Vivian's eyes as the eventual heir to Clyne.

Algernon came from a military family. His father had made his career in the 8th Hussars, fought in the Crimea, and so distinguished himself during the Indian Mutiny that he was awarded the Victoria Cross. His kinsman and godfather was Admiral Sir Algernon Heneage, under whom the heir of Clyne began his naval career in 1886 as a midshipman on the old masted battleship, *H.M.S. Triumph*, Heneage's flagship on the Pacific station. Algernon was to follow closely in his relative's footsteps and, with great credit, he too rose to the rank of full admiral by 1927.

Algernon was privately educated at Evelyn's and Stubbington until, at the age of fifteen, he was sent to sea. His apprenticeship with Admiral Heneage completed, he had joined the crew of *H.M.S. Royal Arthur* in the Pacific before 1892 as a lieutenant and spent much of his time learning the new techniques of anti-submarine warfare, in which he was to be an expert throughout his career. On the *Royal Arthur* he qualified in torpedo duties and was appointed torpedo-lieutenant on the brand new cruiser, *H.M.S. Powerful*, in 1892. He was promoted commander in May 1900 when he was just twenty-nine, a rapid promotion by any standard. Algernon accompanied the ship to north China in 1897 and witnessed many of the events that led to the Boxer uprising against European lives and interests in the Chinese Empire. From there, in 1899, the *Powerful* made for South Africa on a mission to assist the British land forces in the Boer War; on the way, he observed the fighting in the Spanish-American campaigns in the Phillipines. Indeed, Algernon was to be present at some of the most critical encounters of his day and would play a significant role in some of them.

PLATE 36 *Captain Walker-Heneage about the time of the outbreak of war in 1914.*

Mr. C. Fraser Jenkins

PLATE 37 *Rear-Admiral Walker-Heneage at the end of the First World War.*
Mr. C. Fraser Jenkins

His particular contribution in South Africa was of considerable importance. At the siege of Ladysmith he was second-in-command of the naval contingent sent ashore at Durban with guns from the *Powerful* to assist in the defence of the town, on whose relief the fate of the British Empire seemed for a moment to depend. The fighting qualities of this young lieutenant and the naval gunners accompanying him were later said to have contributed materially to the defence of Ladysmith, and Algernon was duly mentioned in despatches. The naval contingent's operation lasted four months from the end of October 1899; at each shot of its guns the Zulus present danced and laughed. *Powerful* then set sail for home with Algernon seriously ill with dysentery and enteric contracted during the siege.

By 1 January 1907 he was ripe for promotion to captain, and he was given command of *H.M.S. Hyacinth*, one of the first British ships to be equipped for minelaying, with which Captain Walker-Heneage was well familiar. The following year, he served as flag captain to the commander-in-chief, East Indies, in the *Hyacinth*, commanding a squadron of mine-layers. This kind of assignment in one of the newer spheres of modern warfare was to be his major contribution to the Allied effort in the First World War.

Between 1910 and 1914, Algernon was captain of the cruisers *Andromache* and *Naiad* in home waters. He began his wartime service by helping to protect the British Expeditionary Force being transported to France. On 1 August 1914, he had taken command of his first battleship, the veteran *H.M.S. Albion*, and soon afterwards embarked on a secret mission to the south Atlantic. His orders (so it later emerged) were to bring back to Britain gold bullion from the South African mines which was urgently needed to finance the war effort. The cargo, known to the crew simply as 'special ammunition', was successfully shipped to Gibraltar, all 84 tons of it valued at £17 million. It was subsequently reported to the House of Commons that Algernon's mission had been responsible for increasing the country's credit at a critical moment by as much as £40 million. The voyage was intended, too, to protect British merchant shipping in the south Atlantic, and to aid the troops engaged in suppressing the Boer rebellion at Walfish Bay. All this was successfully achieved before the *Albion* steamed into Gibraltar early in February 1915.

New orders awaited Algernon which were to send him into one of the most dangerous theatres of the war – the eastern Mediterranean. There an attempt was about to be made to land Allied troops at Gallipoli in order to undermine Turkish aid to the Germans. The main objective was an ambitious one and Algernon's particular assignment, to help protect the fleet of mine-sweepers in the Dardanelles and assist in the barrage accompanying the landings, proved well-nigh impossible. The *Albion* suffered heavy damage and grievous casualties. But confidence in Captain Walker-Heneage was unshaken. As commodore in command of a flotilla of small vessels, including 160 minesweepers, his mission to clear the sea of floating mines so that the Allied fleet could pass the Straits of Salamis was conducted with great courage under constant bombardment. In August 1916, the commodore in *H.M.S. Hussar* was partly responsible for the demonstration before Athens which helped to bring to power in Greece a government better disposed towards the Allies than that of King Constantine. In order to blockade the Austrian fleet in the Adriatic and prevent its submarines from slipping out, in 1917 he assembled his boats again to place the 'Otranto Net' across the entrance to the sea, though it proved a forlorn task. Twice he was mentioned in despatches (Plates 36, 37).

At the end of the war, Algernon, now a rear-admiral, was senior British naval officer in Italy. He retired from active service in 1920, just before the death of his aged aunt Dulcie; he no doubt realised that the Clyne estate in Swansea would soon demand his attention (Plate 38). Nevertheless, his naval promotion continued, first to vice-admiral in 1923 and then full admiral in 1927. His had been a distinguished career, even though he had decided to retire early at the age of forty-nine. The orders and decorations bestowed on him reflect the esteem in which he was held by foreign governments as well as his own. In 1904, after escorting Queen Alexandra on one of her many visits to Scandinavia, he was made a member of the Victorian Order, and in 1916 a Commander of the Order of the Bath. From the French government he received the Légion d'Honneur, from the Japanese the Order of the Rising Sun (second class), and from Italy the Order of Grand Officer of the Crown of Italy (Plates 39, 40).

PLATE 38 *Rear-Admiral Walker-Heneage at the time of Dulcie Vivian's death in 1921.*

Mr. C. Fraser Jenkins

PLATE 39 *Vice-Admiral Walker-Heneage-Vivian in full dress uniform with decorations, from the painting by Evan Walters, 1926.*
Glynn Vivian Art Gallery and University College of Swansea

In 1920 Algernon moved back to Parc le Breos, the estate which Graham Vivian had left him for life (or until he inherited Clyne), together with an annuity of £7,000. Within a year, Dulcie Vivian was dead and Algernon came into the entire Clyne inheritance as a life tenant. He fulfilled his uncle's instructions to the letter, adding Vivian to his name and securing royal licence to adopt the arms of Vivian on 21 July 1921 (Plate 41).

Unlike Graham, Algernon entered fully into the society of the Swansea area, though his contacts with London, with politicians and other influential people were maintained. He took a place on the board of the family business, Vivian and Sons Ltd., and eventually became its chairman. This alone would have made him a much sought-after personage by local organisations. Moreover, his wartime career disposed him to accept the Honorary Colonelcy of the 53rd (Welsh) Division Training R.A.S.C. (T), and patronage of the Swansea branch of the British Legion – and perhaps, too, the post of County Commissioner of the Scout Movement. Reunions, especially of the Ladysmith campaign, delighted him. His business interests took him to the chairmanship of the Trustee Savings Bank in Swansea and to the board of trustees of Swansea Hospital, to which his uncle and aunt had been generous in their time. And he was a willing chairman of Swansea Cricket and Football Club. Despite his strong conservative instincts he played only a formal role in party politics, becoming in 1921 chairman and subsequently president of the Gower Conservative Association. Like Graham Vivian before him, he was elected in his turn high sheriff of Glamorgan (1926), a J.P. and deputy-lieutenant of the county. As the owner of a substantial estate, Algernon showed the same interest in the wild life of the countryside as his uncle. And above all, he shared Graham Vivian's passion for the horticultural development of Clyne Park, even sponsoring expeditions abroad to acquire rare species of seed. He was a prominent member of the Rhododendron Society, and a founder and first president of the Gower Society which, ever since, has devoted itself to the protection of the peninsula's natural beauties.

Soon after he came into his inheritance, Algernon decided to sell 7 Belgrave Square (for he had his own house in Hyde Park Gardens). But the Clyne estate was kept intact throughout his lifetime, with very minor modification. In October 1921, for example, perhaps taking advantage of his recent inheritance of the estate from Dulcie Vivian, the Town Council approached him to sell a small piece of land fronting the Mumbles Road in order to widen the carriageway. It was the kind of proposal to evoke an uncompromising 'no' from Graham Vivian; Algernon sold the property for £348. He changed the aspect of the estate in small ways only; the small look-out tower that stands above the castle to the west was built to enable him to survey his treasured rhododendrons and to gaze, telescope in hand, at the sea

PLATE 40 *Admiral Walker-Heneage-Vivian, from the painting by Margaret Lindsay Williams, 1931.*

Mrs. B. Heneage-Williams

and the ships he had forsaken. When Algernon died, his estates were more than 2,600 acres in extent, divided between the Clyne and Parc le Breos properties of Graham Vivian. The pheasants, duck and wood pigeons of Clyne were still famous, and in the inter-war years the Admiral's shoots attracted statesmen, soldiers, naval officers, aristocrats and bishops. The prince of Wales (later King Edward VIII) stayed at Clyne; so did Neville Chamberlain, Stanley Baldwin, and other Conservative politicians, among whom Winston Churchill had the quaint distinction of having one of the more capacious of Clyne's baths named after him (Plates 42, 43, 44).

Their host was an entertaining man, with a career full of interest and personal qualities that made him a striking individualist. He had a well developed sense of humour, even a mischievous sense of fun. Despite the urgency of the mission to South Africa in 1914, Captain Walker-Heneage entered into the spirit of the age-old celebrations to mark the *Albion's* crossing of the equator. He and King Neptune dispensed with the customary 'order of the bath' for those crossing the line for the first time, but in his speech (recorded verbatim by a marine on board) the captain rose to the occasion magnificently:

> Your Majesty, as an ancient subject I gladly welcome you to this good ship and observe with pleasure that it is 27 years almost to a day since I was first presented to your Majesty almost on the self same spot on board the saucy 'Espeigle', and that since then perhaps my beard and those of your many other old subjects may have grown longer yet you seem to take no note of time and your beautiful Queen looks as young and coquettish as ever and her complexion wears well considering the watery nature of her home. You will, I hope, recognise very many in this ship who like myself have been presented before and have received the gentle attention of your followers, for we in this ship are no company of boys who sail on his Britannic Majesty's waters in this time of war. I beg your Majesties to pardon our hasty reception as we pass the line which divides your kingdom, but our business is urgent to drive from the seas those who wish to wrest from Britannia her hold on the Trident and who if they had it would hold it with a 'mailed fist' rather

PLATE 41 *The arms of Algernon Walker-Heneage-Vivian, as authorised by King George V in 1921.*

A copy from the records of the College of Arms, by permission of Collins, Woods and Vaughan Jones, solicitors

than with a tarry hand. . . .

A year later, in July 1915, Captain Walker-Heneage encountered the novelist and humorist, Compton Mackenzie, on the island of Tenedos, just south of the Dardanelles. There is no more eloquent testimony to the captain's brisk and playful sense of humour than that he was able to amuse Mackenzie. As Algernon hurried ashore, he appeared 'a tall lanky man on wires, hair as long, that morning at any rate, as a painter's or a veteran politican's'.

'Come to take you away', he shouted to Captain Loring (then governor of Tenedos).

'Where to?'

'You've been given the *Albion*. I've brought a new governor with me, and I can give you exactly one hour to pack.'

While they were waiting, Mackenzie entertained Captain Heneage, or to be accurate I was entertained by him. He was the Commodore in command of all the small vessels in these waters, and was known as Captain K. in the same way as the Commodore of the destroyer flotilla was known as Captain D. 'Can you guess why I call them ketches instead of trawlers', Captain K. asked me. 'Why, I'll tell you. I call them ketches so that when I'm asked for a trawler I can always reply with perfect truth that I haven't got a single one to spare.'

At this he walked rapidly up and down the quay, shouting with laughter at such an ingenious device for sidetracking exigent admirals.

It was an incident that stuck in the mind of Compton Mackenzie, who recorded it in his memoirs of the Gallipoli campaign. Yet to members of his own family Algernon could be a stern father and to those who served under him a demanding commander. On the way to South Africa, *H.M.S. Albion* put in at Gibraltar on 1 September 1914. Some of the crew on shore-leave got drunk and a patrol sent to keep order returned in the same condition. Next morning, a marine on board recorded in his diary that the 'lot of fatheads had a lecture from the Captain on last night's goings on'. But he could also be appreciative of the harsh conditions under which his men worked and he duly complimented them for enduring the intense heat of

PLATE 42 *Winston Churchill at Clyne Castle as a guest of the Admiral (centre right).*

Mrs. B. Heneage-Williams

PLATE 43 *The visit of the Prince of Wales (later King Edward VIII) (third left) to Clyne Castle, with the Admiral (extreme left).*

Mrs. B. Heneage-Williams

their voyage south and for their gunnery in the Dardanelles engagements later on. The eccentricity he allowed himself stemmed from the ineradicable habits of a naval captain: he was an inveterate and fastidious note-taker, diarist and account-keeper – whether he was planning his plantings at Clyne, recording his journeys to London and elsewhere, or keeping a tally of his income and expenditure. The log continued to be kept on dry land.

The Admiral had no sons but three daughters by his first wife, Helen, eldest daughter of Captain Ernest de Vismes du Boulay; he had married her in 1912. This fact and the estate-duty legislation of post-war governments at last successfully thwarted the carefully-laid plans of Graham Vivian. When Algernon died on 26 February 1952, after two months of ailing health, a high proportion of his estate – about two thirds of it (compared with less than one-sixth of Graham's when he died in 1912) was claimed by the Chancellor of the Exchequer. Had he survived another nine weeks, the estate would have qualified under existing legislation for a considerably lower rate of duty and it might have survived and passed to another of Graham Vivian's descendants. But in February 1952, there was no alternative but to dispose of the castle, much of its contents, and the property in order to meet the debt. This was undertaken in September 1952.

PLATE 44 *The Admiral meeting the prime minister, Stanley Baldwin, at Swansea Station en route for Clyne Castle, 1923.*

Mrs. B. Heneage-Williams

Town and University

The decision of Swansea Town Council to purchase part of the Clyne estate after the death of Admiral Walker-Heneage-Vivian seems to have been taken in a hurry. As late as 2 September 1952, less than a month before the sale was due to be held at the Mackworth Hotel, Swansea, an enquiry was made of the Council's likely attitude to the establishment of a Roman Catholic secondary school for girls at Clyne Castle. Those who made the enquiry were assured informally that there was no obstacle to securing planning permission. A fortnight later, on 17 September, the Council approved the purchase of the castle and its park under compulsory purchase legislation. Some months afterwards, an Independent member of the Council, stirring his constituents at election time, was to claim that pressure had been exerted to block the Roman Catholic plan by using the compulsory purchase powers of the Council. However accurate this suggestion (and such anti-Catholic sentiment is embedded in the nonconformist consciousness of south Wales), other uses for the castle were being mooted in the town. At the end of September, therefore, the castle and seventy-six acres of neighbouring land were withdrawn from the sale on the instructions of the Town Council. They were purchased for Swansea early in 1953 for £17,500.

Proposals for the future of Clyne were hurriedly solicited by the Council once the purchase had been made. For one thing, the condition of the house would deteriorate in the winter and spring, while by the summer the rich wildlife of the estate, no longer controlled by the Admiral's shoots, was already proving a nuisance to people living nearby. The proposals that were forthcoming ranged from the socially desirable to the distinctly bizarre. The social needs of a town which had suffered horribly in the Second World War would undoubtedly have been well served if, as was suggested, the castle and its grounds had been turned into a school for the handicapped, a residential centre for adult education, a convalescent home or a maternity centre. Considerations of prestige were behind the proposal that the castle should become the residence of the mayor and the assize judges. The town's treasurer was, understandably, more interested in the commercial prospects, and favoured converting it into a first-class hotel. Somewhat stranger were the suggestions that the castle should become a crematorium and the park an extravaganza of a zoological garden, with a circus, dancing platform, aquarium and a battery of slot machines. The proposal which met with greatest favour, and was supported by members of the University College, was to establish at Clyne either a folk museum on the distinguished model of St. Fagans, or an industrial and science museum. At first, the Council itself was impressed with this prospect. But the discussion was overtaken from an unexpected quarter.

The principal and registrar of the University College of Swansea had been showing informal interest in Clyne Castle for some time. In November 1952, soon after the compulsory purchase order had been issued, confidential discussions had been held between the clerk of the Town Council, T. B. Bowen, and Principal J. S. (later Lord) Fulton of the University College. In Bowen and Alderman Percy Morris, M.P. for Swansea West and chairman of the Council's Parliamentary Committee, the College had sympathetic advocates in the Guildhall, although the negotiations between the two organisations were not unruffled. The College's hope was that the castle would be converted into a hall of residence for men. University education was on the threshold of rapid expansion and yet Swansea's College still had only one hall of residence – and that for women. The University Grants Committee under its chairman, Sir Arthur Trueman, who knew Swansea well as its first professor of geology, encouraged the idea and during 1953 the informal negotiations proceeded satisfactorily – until November.

As with most University towns, in the 1950s there existed in Swansea in some quarters a distrust of the University College and a suspicion that its expansionist

PLATE 45 *An aerial view of Clyne Castle and its grounds taken in 1919.*   Mrs. B. Heneage-Williams

plans would prejudice the Council's own post-war proposals and deprive the townsfolk of some of their amenities. These sentiments were shared by a few of the councillors, who maintained that the College showed no interest in the Borough and that the Borough had none in the College. At a late stage in the discussion, therefore, an attempt was made in November 1953 to suspend negotiations with the College. The Council was induced to advertise in the press for other proposals for the future use of Clyne. None was forthcoming and the opposition to the College's plans could be sustained no longer. Negotiations were resumed in January 1954 and had reached their penultimate stage by April. Decisive backing by the University Grants Committee, whose new chairman paid a personal visit to Clyne in May, enabled the College to propose the outright sale of Clyne Castle to the College. This was eventually accepted by the Town Council in the spring of 1955 and the price was set at £12,751. The cost of conversion into a hall of residence was estimated to be in the region of £130,000.

The residual hostility towards the College's acquisition of the site broke the surface occasionally in later months, but a highly satisfactory agreement was eventually reached. The remarkable park created by Graham Vivian and the Admiral was preserved for the people of Swansea and was opened to the public at Easter 1954. The castle was unobtrusively converted into a student residence by the University College. Two further small plots were purchased nearby in 1964 and 1966, when plans were being finalised for a second, entirely modern, hall of residence adjacent to the castle. When that building was opened in 1968, the College's development at Clyne was complete.

In the castle, the College acquired a capital asset of architectural and historical importance as well as an unrivalled site for a hall of residence. The original idea owed much to the vision of Principal Fulton, and the happy outcome of the lengthy negotiations are a tribute to the patience and skill of the principal and the registrar, John MacIntyre. The College subsequently showed itself to be fully aware of the heritage it had acquired in 1955. Parts of the building were then 150 years old, and during the Second World War some of the larger rooms had been rarely used. Moreover, for three years before the purchase the castle had stood empty. In these circumstances, it was inevitable that the fabric of Clyne should begin to deteriorate markedly. Even before the purchase was completed, the College spent £7,000 on making the old building 'wind and weather-tight'. Afterwards, major renovations were undertaken, whilst the alterations to the fine rooms of the house were kept to a minimum. Great care was taken lest the rare trees, shrubs and plants should be damaged or moved, and hence the rhododendrons, magnolias, fuchsias, Scotch pines, palm trees, cherry and cedar trees still stand much as they have done since Graham Vivian's day. The oak-panelled doors and carved, gilded overdoors were retained almost throughout the building and their paintwork has been subsequently refurbished. The unique, curved drawing-room has become the library of the hall, and the lofty Great Hall its junior common room. The dining-room constructed by Graham Vivian in the 1860s does the same duty today as it did then. Only the tapestry room has disappeared.

It might be thought surprising that the University College did not preserve the name of Vivian when it renamed the castle as a hall of residence. But it then seemed more appropriate to commemorate the man who, more than any other, had been instrumental in founding a University College in Swansea in 1920, F. W. Gilbertson. Frank Gilbertson was a steel and tinplate magnate, one of a family of industrialists who had created the engineering town of Pontardawe in the second half of the nineteenth century. He became the first president of University College, Swansea, in 1920. His daughter married Captain Hugh Vivian, a nephew of Graham and a cousin of the Admiral.

Neuadd Gilbertson (Gilbertson Hall) welcomed its first students in 1956. At the official opening, in the presence of Lord Tenby, then president of the University College, and Sir Keith Murray, the chairman of the U.G.C. who had sustained Principal Fulton in his plans, Sir Lewis Jones described it with justifiable pride as 'one of the finest halls of residence in the country'. Graham Vivian would certainly not have dissented (Plates 45, 46, Rear cover).

PLATE 46 *An aerial view of Clyne Castle as part of the University College's hall of residence, taken in 1956.* University College of Swansea

Conclusion

The Clyne estate was the creation of enterprising newcomers to Swansea. The Phillips family came from Carmarthenshire, the Wardes from Kent, Graham Vivian was of Cornish stock, and the Admiral was in part a Wiltshire man. Not one of them was a farmer or made any serious effort to cultivate the estate himself. The two men who left the greatest mark on the house were Warde and Vivian, whose pockets were well lined with the profits of industry which they lavished on the house and its estate, Vivian more bounteously than Warde. Nevertheless, the history of Woodlands and Clyne is the chronicle of the dangers which could face ambitious landowners and the descendants of pioneer industrialists in the nineteenth and early-twentieth centuries. None of the owners of the property, with the single exception of Graham Vivian, ultimately had sufficient resources with which to maintain the pretensions they cherished for Clyne. Warde died heavily in debt, the Berringtons were driven to demolish part of the house to make ends meet, and the Admiral ultimately fell victim to post-war advances in social equality. The millionaire Graham, the shrewd businessman, was the only one who died possessed of assets far in excess of those he had himself inherited.

Each of the owners of Clyne interested himself closely in the industrial development of the town of Swansea and in the quality of its life. The Vivians were pre-eminent among those who brought the town world renown, and Dulcie was probably more generous than most with her charitable gifts in difficult times.

It is striking, too, that none of the families at Clyne established a dynasty of squires there. Vivian occupied the house longest, for more than fifty years, and in that time succeeded in attracting the regard of his contemporaries as well as of his tenants as 'The Squire of Clyne'. He had no children of his own and neither did his sister Dulcie, but by an astute device he hoped to be able to perpetuate the name of Vivian at Clyne. After rather less than a century, the Vivians surrendered the core of their estate to the town of Swansea. Neither the Phillipses, whose business was in London, nor the Wardes, who could not afford to keep the castle in the family, nor the Berringtons, who were only too happy to sell in 1859, created a line of squires at Clyne. The house and the estate were very much personal creations of George Warde and William Graham Vivian. Their mark is still clearly discernible at Clyne, and in the hands of the University College the fabric of their castle has been carefully preserved.

Acknowledgements

In my pursuit of the history of Clyne Castle and its owners, I have been helped along the way by a number of people who responded generously to my enquiries. I offer my sincere thanks to them all.

Photographs were provided or authorised by several institutions and private individuals: in Swansea, by the Royal Institution of South Wales, the Central Public Library, the Glynn Vivian Art Gallery, the City Archives Office and, of course, the University College; at Aberystwyth, the National Library of Wales; in Cardiff, Thomson Newspapers; in London, the British Library and the National Portrait Gallery; and by Mr. Rowley Davies, Miss Maxwell Fraser, Mrs. C. D. Fraser Jenkins, Mr. C. Fraser Jenkins, Mrs. B. Heneage-Williams, Mr. John Warde and Mr. E. G. Wright. Mr. Roger Davies of the University College of Swansea took other photographs, including those from documents in the possession of Collins, Woods and Vaughan Jones, solicitors, of Swansea. Dr. Roger Thomas of the University College of Swansea made others available to me. Permission to reproduce some of these photographs in this booklet is gratefully acknowledged.

Mr. David Bevan, archivist of the University College of Swansea, afforded me access to a number of manuscripts, including the W. G. Vivian Collection, which has been usefully listed by Mrs. Margaret Walker. At the National Library of Wales, Mr. R. W. McDonald guided me through the largely unsorted Vivian (Lord Swansea) Papers. At the Berkshire Record Office, I was able to consult General Warde's letters (some of them written at Woodlands Castle) to the Stevens family of Bradfield. Mr. Hugh Morgan of Collins, Woods and Vaughan Jones arranged for me to consult other material relating to Graham Vivian and Admiral Walker-Heneage-Vivian. Through the good offices of Mr. Morgan and his colleague, Mr. Stuart Batcup, I was able to meet Mrs. C. D. Fraser Jenkins, one of the Admiral's daughters, and Mrs. Beryl Heneage-Williams, his widow: both were gracious hosts and helpful in answering questions and giving me sight of personal possessions; in Mrs. Heneage-Williams's case, the Ladysmith Diary kept by the Admiral and the Visitors' Books of Clyne Castle dating from 1887 are unique historical documents. The Admiral's grandson, Mr. Christopher Fraser Jenkins, provided valuable photographs and allowed me to read his grandfather's brief autobiography, written in 1929 for the information of his daughters.

My colleague, Dr. John Hayward, placed his unrivalled knowledge of Clyne Park and its contents at my disposal, and interesting reminiscences were forthcoming from Mr. G. I. Govier, formerly employed by the Admiral as a mason and the verger of Clyne Chapel for upwards of fifty years, and from Mr. E. G. Wright, whose father was head gardener at Clyne for a number of years under Graham and Dulcie Vivian and the Admiral. Mr. G. E. Jones's 'An outline history of Clyne Castle', which appeared in Neuadd Gilbertson's magazine, *The New Clynian,* in 1960, provided valuable details, including the reminiscences of Mr. A. G. Court, who was in the Admiral's employ in 1952. Dr. John Alban, archivist of the city of Swansea, and Mr. A. N. F. Rees, its chief executive, allowed me to consult the records of the former Town Council and its clerk, Mr. T. B. Bowen; and at the University College, Dr. Roger Thomas, on behalf of the College Officers, placed the correspondence of Principal J. S. Fulton at my disposal.

Other useful information was provided by Mr. Howell Mendus, Mr. Ray Stevens, and Mr. John Hughes, local studies librarian of West Glamorgan County Council; the Royal Commission on Ancient and Historical Monuments in Wales and Monmouthshire, the Public Record Office, Cardiff Public Library, and the National Army Museum, London. The letters of a midshipman and the diary kept by a marine on board *H.M.S. Albion* in 1914–16 may be consulted at the Imperial War Museum, London.

My interest in the castle was first aroused when I served

as sub-warden of Neuadd Gilbertson in 1966–69; since then I have been allowed to wander at will through the buildings by the indulgence of successive wardens and Miss Sally Roberts, until recently the Hall's matron. The Rev. A. E. Pierce and Mr. Govier gave me permission to examine Clyne Chapel. I am indebted, too, to my friends, Dr. Prys Morgan, Dr. Roger Thomas and Professor Glanmor Williams, who read a draft of this eassy and improved it in a number of ways; and to Mr. G. B. Lewis, who drew the maps. Finally, I am grateful to the principal, registrar and officers of the University College of Swansea for the opportunity to write this booklet and for encouraging its completion. Dr. Roger Thomas, of the registrar's department, brought me periodically back to the task when my mind wandered elsewhere, and ensured its smooth passage towards publication.